The Forgotten Conflict: The Korean War's Enduring Impact on History

Copyright Page

TITLE: The Forgotten Conflict: The Korean War's Enduring Impact on History

1ST Edition

ISBN: 9798223380894

Table of Contents

The Forgotten Conflict: The Korean War's Enduring Impact on History

By Roberto Miguel Rodriguez

Chapter 1: The Korean War: The War That Has Not Ended

The Origins of the Korean War

The Korean War, often referred to as the "Forgotten Conflict," is a pivotal event in history that continues to have a profound impact on the world today. Understanding its origins is crucial to comprehending the complexities and enduring implications of this war.

The Korean War was sparked by a series of events that occurred in the aftermath of World War II. With the defeat of Japan in 1945, Korea, which had been under Japanese colonial rule since 1910, was liberated. However, the country soon found itself divided along the 38th parallel, with the Soviet Union occupying the north and the United States occupying the south.

Tensions escalated as both occupying powers sought to establish separate governments in their respective regions. In 1948, this culminated in the formation of two separate Korean states: the communist Democratic People's Republic of Korea (DPRK) in the north, and the capitalist Republic of Korea (ROK) in the south. The division of Korea became a symbol of the global ideological struggle between communism and capitalism, with the Cold War intensifying.

The origins of the Korean War can also be traced to the role of propaganda. Both sides engaged in a war of words, demonizing each other and portraying themselves as the rightful government of a unified Korea. This propaganda played a significant role in fueling the conflict and shaping public opinion both domestically and internationally.

External powers also exerted a substantial influence on the Korean War. The Soviet Union provided military support to the communist North, while the United States supported the capitalist South. These external powers not only supplied weapons and troops but also shaped the strategies and objectives of the warring factions.

The experiences of Korean prisoners of war (POWs) during and after the war were harrowing. Many endured inhumane treatment, including torture and forced labor. The plight of these POWs and the challenges they faced upon their release have left a lasting impact on the collective memory of the Korean people.

The Korean War also brought about significant cultural and societal changes in North and South Korea. The war disrupted traditional social structures, leading to the rise of new social movements and ideologies. Women played a crucial role in the war effort, serving as nurses, factory workers, and even soldiers, challenging gender norms and contributing to the feminist movement in both countries.

The legacy of the Korean War extends beyond the Korean Peninsula. The war's impact on international relations and geopolitics is undeniable. It marked a turning point in the Cold War, solidifying the division between communist and capitalist blocs and shaping the global order for decades to come.

The economic consequences of the Korean War were immense. Both North and South Korea suffered significant damage to their infrastructure and economies. The war also resulted in the loss of countless lives and the displacement of millions of people, creating a humanitarian crisis that still resonates today.

The United Nations played a critical role in the Korean War, with its intervention on behalf of the South. This marked the first time the international organization took military action to resolve a conflict, setting a precedent for future peacekeeping missions.

Lastly, the Korean War was plagued by numerous human rights violations. Both sides committed atrocities, including massacres, sexual violence, and forced displacement of civilians. These violations continue to be a source of pain and trauma for the Korean people.

In conclusion, understanding the origins of the Korean War is essential to grasp the war's enduring impact on history. From the role of propaganda and external powers to the experiences of POWs and the cultural and societal changes that followed, this conflict has left an indelible mark on the Korean Peninsula and the world at large. From its economic consequences to its legacy on international relations and human rights, the Korean War remains an ongoing topic of study and reflection for historians.

The Divisions and Alliances

The Korean War was a conflict that not only had lasting implications for the Korean Peninsula but also had a profound impact on the course of history. This chapter explores the divisions and alliances that emerged during the war and their enduring consequences.

At the heart of the Korean War were the divisions between North and South Korea. The war originated from the ideological divide between communism and capitalism, with the North backed by the Soviet Union and China, and the South supported by the United States and its allies. These alliances further deepened the divisions and turned Korea into a proxy battleground for the Cold War powers.

Propaganda played a crucial role in shaping public opinion during the Korean War. Both sides utilized various mediums to promote their cause and demonize their adversaries. The chapter delves into the role of propaganda and its impact on shaping public perception of the war, both domestically and internationally.

One of the most enduring consequences of the Korean War was the division of the Korean Peninsula. The war led to the establishment of a demilitarized zone that still exists today, dividing families and perpetuating tensions between North and South Korea. This subchapter explores the impact of the war on the division and its lasting effects on the Korean people.

External powers, particularly the United States and the Soviet Union, played an influential role in the Korean War. The chapter examines the motivations and actions of these powers, as well as their impact on the course and outcome of the conflict.

The experiences of Korean prisoners of war (POWs) during and after the war are another crucial aspect explored in this subchapter. It delves into the treatment of POWs, the challenges they faced upon their release, and the long-term psychological and social consequences of their captivity.

The Korean War brought about significant cultural and societal changes in both North and South Korea. This subchapter investigates the transformations that occurred in these societies as a result of the war, including changes in gender roles, education, and the economy.

Furthermore, this chapter examines the legacy of the Korean War on international relations and geopolitics. The war had far-reaching consequences, shaping the global balance of power and influencing future conflicts.

The economic consequences of the Korean War are also explored in this subchapter. The war devastated both North and South Korea, leading to economic hardships that persisted long after the fighting ceased.

The role of the United Nations in the Korean War is another important aspect that this chapter addresses. It explores the UN's involvement in the conflict and the challenges it faced in maintaining peace and stability.

Lastly, this subchapter delves into the human rights violations that occurred during the Korean War. It sheds light on the atrocities committed by all sides and the impact they had on the Korean people.

In conclusion, "The Divisions and Alliances" subchapter provides a comprehensive analysis of the various aspects of the Korean War, addressing the interests of historians and the niches of The Korean War, propaganda, the Korean Peninsula's division, external powers, POW experiences, cultural changes, women's role, legacy on international relations, economic consequences, UN's role, and human rights violations. It offers a deep understanding of the war's enduring impact on history and its multifaceted consequences.

The Armistice Agreement

The Armistice Agreement signed on July 27, 1953, marked the end of the Korean War, a conflict that has had a profound and enduring impact on history. This subchapter explores the significance of the Armistice Agreement in relation to various aspects of the Korean War and its aftermath.

One of the primary themes discussed in relation to the Armistice Agreement is the role of propaganda in the Korean War. Historians have analyzed the ways in which both sides utilized propaganda to shape public opinion and gain support for their cause. The signing of the Armistice Agreement presented a unique opportunity for both North and South Korea to create narratives that justified their actions and reinforced their respective ideologies.

Furthermore, the Armistice Agreement had a direct impact on the division of the Korean Peninsula. The agreement led to the establishment of the Demilitarized Zone (DMZ) as a buffer zone between North and South Korea. This division, which remains to this day, has had profound social, economic, and political consequences for the Korean people and the region as a whole.

The influence of external powers in the Korean War is another significant aspect explored in relation to the Armistice Agreement. The involvement of major powers such as the United States, China, and the Soviet Union shaped the course of the war and ultimately influenced the terms of the Armistice Agreement. Understanding these external influences is crucial to comprehending the geopolitical dynamics that have persisted in the region since the war's end.

The experiences of Korean prisoners of war (POWs) during and after the conflict are also examined in relation to the Armistice Agreement. The agreement detailed the repatriation of POWs, but many faced significant challenges upon their return to their respective countries. The subchapter delves into the stories of these individuals, shedding light on their struggles and the long-lasting impact of their captivity.

Furthermore, the subchapter explores the cultural and societal changes that occurred in North and South Korea after the war. The Korean War not only left physical scars on the peninsula but also brought about significant transformations in the cultural and social fabric of both nations.

Finally, the subchapter examines the legacy of the Korean War on international relations, geopolitics, human rights, and the global economy. The Armistice Agreement was a pivotal moment in shaping these aspects, and understanding its consequences is crucial for comprehending the lasting impact of the Korean War on the world stage.

In conclusion, the Armistice Agreement is a critical milestone in the history of the Korean War. This subchapter delves into its significance in relation to various aspects of the conflict and its aftermath, providing historians with a comprehensive understanding of the enduring impact of the war and its far-reaching consequences.

The Ongoing Conflict and its Implications

The Korean War, often referred to as the "Forgotten Conflict," holds an enduring impact on history. In this subchapter, we will delve into the ongoing conflict and its implications, shedding light on various aspects that have shaped the Korean Peninsula and influenced international relations and geopolitics. This chapter aims to provide historians with a comprehensive understanding of the multifaceted consequences of the Korean War.

Firstly, we will explore the war that has not ended, examining the reasons behind the continued division of the Korean Peninsula. Despite the signing of an armistice in 1953, the absence of a formal peace treaty has perpetuated tensions between North and South Korea, resulting in an ongoing state of conflict. We will analyze the factors contributing to this prolonged division and the implications it has had on the Korean people.

Propaganda played a significant role in the Korean War, shaping public opinion and mobilizing support for the respective factions. By delving into the role of propaganda, we will uncover the techniques employed by both sides and their impact on the war's outcome. Understanding this aspect is crucial in comprehending the complexities of the conflict.

External powers played a pivotal role in the Korean War, with the involvement of countries like the United States, China, and the Soviet Union. We will examine the influence exerted by these powers and their motivations behind supporting either North or South Korea. By analyzing their involvement, we can better comprehend the global dimensions of this conflict.

The experiences of Korean prisoners of war (POWs) during and after the war are another critical aspect to explore. We will shed light on the treatment of POWs, their struggles, and their reintegration into society. Understanding the plight of these individuals provides us with valuable insights into the human impact of the war and its aftermath.

Furthermore, we will explore the cultural and societal changes that occurred in North and South Korea post-war. The Korean War had a profound influence on the social fabric of both nations, leading to transformations in various aspects of life. By examining these changes, we can gain a deeper understanding of the long-lasting consequences of the conflict.

The role of women in the Korean War is another aspect that deserves attention. We will explore the contributions made by women on the front lines, as well as the social changes that occurred as a result. This analysis will help us appreciate the significant role played by women during times of conflict.

The legacy of the Korean War on international relations and geopolitics cannot be understated. We will delve into the long-term effects on the global stage, examining how the war shaped alliances, rivalries, and the geopolitical landscape in East Asia.

Additionally, we will explore the economic consequences of the Korean War and its impact on the development of both North and South Korea. This analysis will shed light on the economic disparities that arose and the subsequent challenges faced by these nations.

The role of the United Nations in the Korean War is another crucial aspect to analyze. We will examine the UN's involvement, its successes, and its limitations in resolving the conflict. Understanding the UN's role provides valuable insights into the dynamics of international cooperation during times of crisis.

Lastly, we will address the human rights violations that occurred during the Korean War. By examining the atrocities committed and the impact on civilians, we can gain a deeper understanding of the ethical dimensions of this conflict.

In conclusion, this subchapter aims to provide historians with a comprehensive analysis of the ongoing conflict and its implications. By exploring various aspects such as propaganda, external powers, POW experiences, cultural changes, women's role, international relations, economics, the UN's involvement, and human rights violations, we can gain a more nuanced understanding of the Korean War and its enduring impact on history.

Chapter 2: The Role of Propaganda in the Korean War

Propaganda Techniques and Strategies

Propaganda played a pivotal role in shaping the narrative and outcome of the Korean War. This subchapter aims to shed light on the various techniques and strategies employed by both sides, as well as the impact they had on the course of the conflict and its enduring legacy.

From the outset of the war, propaganda became a powerful weapon in the hands of the belligerents. The North Korean regime, under the leadership of Kim Il-sung, skillfully utilized propaganda to instill a sense of loyalty and fervor among its troops and civilians. Through techniques such as demonization, dehumanization, and the glorification of their own cause, the North Korean regime sought to maintain control over their population and bolster their war effort.

On the other side of the conflict, the United Nations and the United States launched a comprehensive propaganda campaign aimed at rallying support for their cause. They employed techniques such as emotional appeals, patriotic imagery, and the portrayal of North Korea as an aggressive and expansionist state. This propaganda aimed to garner international support for their intervention and legitimize their military actions.

The impact of propaganda on the Korean Peninsula's division cannot be overstated. The demonization of the enemy, coupled with the glorification of one's own cause, further deepened the divide between North and South Korea. The propaganda machinery on both sides perpetuated the notion of ideological and cultural differences, fueling animosity and creating a lasting rift on the Korean Peninsula.

External powers, particularly the Soviet Union and China, also played a significant role in shaping the propaganda landscape of the Korean War. Through their support for North Korea, they utilized propaganda to advance their own geopolitical interests and project their influence in the region.

The experiences of Korean prisoners-of-war (POWs) during and after the conflict were marred by propaganda as well. Both sides attempted to manipulate and exploit POWs for propaganda purposes, often subjecting them to psychological and physical abuse. This subchapter will shed light on the challenges faced by Korean POWs and the long-lasting trauma inflicted upon them.

Additionally, this subchapter will explore the cultural and societal changes that occurred in North and South Korea post-war, as propaganda continued to shape the collective memory and identity of the respective nations. It will also examine the role of women in the Korean War, as they became active participants in propaganda efforts and played crucial roles in supporting the war effort.

The legacy of the Korean War on international relations and geopolitics was profoundly influenced by propaganda. The war set the stage for the Cold War rivalry between the United States and the Soviet Union, transforming the Korean Peninsula into a battleground for their ideological struggle. Propaganda, in turn, became an integral tool in their respective efforts to exert influence over the region.

Furthermore, the economic consequences of the Korean War cannot be overlooked. This subchapter will delve into the propaganda-driven destruction of infrastructure and the long-term economic implications for both North and South Korea.

Lastly, this subchapter will address the human rights violations committed during the Korean War. Propaganda often served as a smokescreen for these violations, as both sides sought to justify their actions through distortion and manipulation of facts.

In conclusion, propaganda techniques and strategies played a significant role in shaping the Korean War and its lasting impact on history. This subchapter aims to provide historians with a comprehensive understanding of how propaganda influenced the war's outcome, the division of the Korean Peninsula, and its enduring legacy on various aspects of the conflict.

Propaganda from North Korea

The Korean War was not only a military conflict but also a battle of ideologies, with propaganda playing a crucial role in shaping the narrative. In this subchapter, we will delve into the propaganda efforts conducted by North Korea during the war and examine their impact on various aspects of the conflict and its aftermath.

North Korea, under the leadership of Kim Il-sung, utilized propaganda as a powerful tool to consolidate his regime's control over the populace and rally support for the war effort. The state-controlled media, such as the Korean Central News Agency and Rodong Sinmun, disseminated a carefully crafted narrative that portrayed North Korea as the victim of aggression and painted their enemies, particularly the United States, as imperialistic invaders. These propaganda efforts aimed to generate a sense of nationalistic fervor and loyalty among the North Korean people, reinforcing the Kim regime's authority.

The impact of North Korean propaganda was far-reaching. Domestically, it helped to maintain social cohesion and foster a cult of personality around Kim Il-sung. The regime's ability to control information enabled it to manipulate public opinion and suppress dissent, ensuring the stability of the regime during and after the war.

Externally, North Korean propaganda aimed to garner international sympathy and support for its cause. By framing the conflict as a struggle against foreign aggression, North Korea sought to rally support from other communist countries and anti-imperialist movements around the world. This propaganda campaign had varying degrees of success, with some nations offering material and moral support to North Korea.

Furthermore, the impact of North Korean propaganda extended beyond the immediate wartime period. The narratives and symbols propagated during the war continued to shape the political landscape of the Korean Peninsula, contributing to the enduring division between North and South Korea. The demonization of the United States and the glorification of the Kim regime became deeply ingrained in North Korean society, making reunification and reconciliation challenging tasks.

In conclusion, the propaganda efforts conducted by North Korea during the Korean War were instrumental in shaping the narratives surrounding the conflict. It played a significant role in maintaining the regime's control domestically, rallying support internationally, and perpetuating the division between North and South Korea. Understanding the power and impact of propaganda in the Korean War is crucial for historians studying the enduring consequences of the conflict, the division of the Korean Peninsula, and the geopolitical dynamics of the region.

Propaganda from South Korea

During the Korean War, propaganda played a significant role in shaping public opinion and garnering support for the respective sides. This subchapter will focus on the propaganda efforts originating from South Korea and their impact on the war.

South Korea, backed by the United States, utilized various propaganda techniques to rally support for their cause and garner international sympathy. One of the key elements of South Korean propaganda was the portrayal of North Korea as a communist aggressor, bent on conquering the entire peninsula. Through vivid and often exaggerated accounts, South Korean propaganda sought to highlight the brutality of the North Korean regime and the threat it posed to the democratic values cherished by the South.

The South Korean government, with the support of the United States, established the Korean Information Service (KIS) to disseminate its propaganda messages. The KIS produced pamphlets, newspapers, and radio broadcasts, which were distributed both domestically and abroad. These materials aimed to demonize the North Korean leadership and depict South Korea as a victim of communist aggression.

One of the most prominent propaganda campaigns from South Korea was the "Movement for the Recovery of the Fatherland." This campaign sought to mobilize the South Korean population, emphasizing the importance of defending their homeland against the communist threat. The campaign utilized various mediums, including posters, slogans, and public rallies, to instill a sense of patriotism and unity among the citizens.

South Korea's propaganda efforts were not limited to the war period alone but extended to the post-war era as well. As the Korean Peninsula remained divided, the South Korean government continued its propaganda campaign, emphasizing the success and prosperity of the democratic South while portraying the North as a poverty-stricken and oppressive regime.

The impact of South Korean propaganda was significant but varied. While it successfully garnered international support for their cause, it also led to the perpetuation of stereotypes and biases against North Korea. The consequences of this propaganda campaign can still be felt today, as it has influenced the ongoing conflict between the two Koreas and shaped international perceptions of the Korean Peninsula.

In conclusion, South Korea's propaganda efforts during the Korean War played a crucial role in shaping public opinion and garnering support for their cause. Through various mediums and campaigns, South Korea sought to portray North Korea as a communist aggressor while emphasizing the importance of defending the democratic values cherished by the South. However, the impact of this propaganda campaign has had enduring consequences on the ongoing conflict and international perceptions of the Korean Peninsula.

International Propaganda Efforts

During the Korean War, international propaganda efforts played a crucial role in shaping the narrative and influencing public opinion. Both sides of the conflict, North Korea and South Korea, as well as their respective allies, employed various strategies to gain support and undermine their opponents. This subchapter explores the pervasive nature of propaganda during the war and its enduring impact on history.

Propaganda was a powerful tool used by all major actors involved in the Korean War. The North Korean regime, led by Kim Il-sung, sought to portray themselves as liberators fighting against American imperialism. They used powerful imagery and rhetoric to rally their own citizens and garner international support. Meanwhile, the South Korean government, backed by the United States and its allies, emphasized the threat of communism and the need to defend democracy. Propaganda was disseminated through various channels, including newspapers, radio broadcasts, and even cultural performances.

External powers also played a significant role in shaping the propaganda narrative. The United States, as the leading anti-communist force, invested heavily in propaganda efforts to counter North Korea's narrative. Hollywood movies, newsreels, and other media platforms were utilized to highlight North Korean atrocities and promote the righteousness of the American cause. Similarly, the Soviet Union and

China supported North Korea through their own propaganda machinery, depicting the conflict as a struggle against Western aggression.

The impact of international propaganda efforts during the Korean War was far-reaching. It not only influenced public opinion at the time but also had lasting effects on the Korean Peninsula's division. The propaganda campaigns served to deepen the ideological divide between North and South Korea, cementing their respective narratives and contributing to the continued hostility between the two nations.

Furthermore, propaganda played a role in the treatment of prisoners of war (POWs) during and after the conflict. Both sides used propaganda to manipulate the treatment of POWs, often subjecting them to indoctrination and coercive tactics. This had long-lasting effects on the experiences of Korean POWs, many of whom faced difficulties reintegrating into society after the war.

In conclusion, international propaganda efforts were a critical aspect of the Korean War, shaping the narrative and influencing public opinion on a global scale. The enduring impact of these efforts can be seen in the continued division of the Korean Peninsula, the experiences of POWs, and the cultural and societal changes in North and South Korea post-war. Understanding the role of propaganda in the Korean War provides valuable insights into the complexities of the conflict and its lasting repercussions on international relations, geopolitics, and human rights.

Chapter 3: The Impact of the Korean War on the Korean Peninsula's Division

The Demilitarized Zone (DMZ)

The Demilitarized Zone (DMZ) is a strip of land that stretches across the Korean Peninsula, dividing North Korea and South Korea. It serves as a buffer zone and a physical barrier between the two countries, a haunting reminder of the Korean War that ended in 1953 with an armistice but no peace treaty.

The DMZ, which is approximately 4 kilometers wide, is heavily fortified and brimming with tension. Landmines, barbed wire, and armed soldiers patrol the area, ensuring that no unauthorized individuals cross the border. Despite its name, the DMZ is far from a peaceful zone, as sporadic military clashes and provocations have occurred throughout the years.

During the Korean War, the DMZ played a crucial role as a battleground between the North and South. It witnessed fierce fighting and witnessed devastating losses on both sides. However, as the war drew to a close, the DMZ became a symbol of the division and the stark contrast between the ideologies and systems of the two countries.

Propaganda has played a significant role in shaping perceptions of the DMZ. Both North and South Korea have used propaganda to promote their respective narratives and justify their actions. The DMZ has become a potent symbol of the ongoing conflict, with both sides attempting to portray themselves as the rightful owners of the entire peninsula.

The DMZ has had a profound impact on the Korean Peninsula's division. It has created a physical and psychological barrier between the two countries, making reunification seem increasingly difficult. The division along the DMZ has resulted in different political, economic, and social systems in North and South Korea, leading to stark differences in living standards and societal values.

External powers have also influenced the DMZ and the Korean War. The involvement of the United States, China, and the Soviet Union during the war and their continued support for North or South Korea have shaped the geopolitical landscape of the region. These external powers have had a stake in the division and have used the DMZ as a bargaining chip in negotiations.

The DMZ has witnessed numerous human rights violations during and after the Korean War. The harsh treatment of prisoners of war (POWs) and the suffering endured by civilians caught in the crossfire have left a lasting impact on the Korean people. The DMZ stands as a grim reminder of the human cost of war and the ongoing violations of human rights.

In conclusion, the Demilitarized Zone (DMZ) is a crucial and complex aspect of the Korean War's enduring impact on history. From its role as a battleground to its representation in propaganda, the DMZ holds significance in various niches of the Korean War's legacy. Its influence on the division of the Korean Peninsula, the involvement of external powers, the experiences of POWs, and its connection to human rights violations all contribute to its importance in understanding the lasting consequences of the war. The DMZ serves as a striking reminder of the unresolved conflict and the challenges that lie ahead for the Korean people and the international community.

Socioeconomic Differences between North and South Korea

The Korean War, which took place from 1950 to 1953, had a profound and lasting impact on the Korean Peninsula, leading to the division of the country into two separate entities: North Korea and South Korea. This subchapter will delve into the socioeconomic differences that emerged between these two regions in the aftermath of the conflict.

One of the most striking differences between North and South Korea is their economic development. While South Korea experienced rapid industrialization and economic growth, becoming one of the world's leading economies, North Korea's economy stagnated under a centralized and planned system. The South Korean government actively pursued market-oriented policies, attracting foreign investment and promoting exports. In contrast, North Korea's economy became heavily reliant on state-controlled industries, resulting in chronic inefficiencies and limited international trade.

The economic consequences of the Korean War played a significant role in shaping these disparities. The war had a devastating impact on both regions, destroying infrastructure and displacing millions of people. However, South Korea received substantial financial aid from the United States and other Western nations, which helped jumpstart its reconstruction efforts. In contrast, North Korea turned to the Soviet Union and China for support, leading to a reliance on foreign aid and a lack of self-sufficiency.

Furthermore, the political ideologies adopted by each region further contributed to their divergent socioeconomic paths. South Korea embraced capitalism and democracy, which fostered a business-friendly environment and encouraged entrepreneurship. On the other hand, North Korea adopted a socialist model and a highly centralized government, inhibiting economic growth and innovation.

These socioeconomic differences also had profound societal and cultural implications. In South Korea, the emphasis on economic development led to significant improvements in living standards, education, and healthcare. The country experienced a rapid urbanization process, with the rise of modern cities and a growing middle class. In contrast, North Korea's economy prioritized military spending and the development of heavy industries, leading to a lower standard of living for its citizens.

In conclusion, the socioeconomic differences between North and South Korea that emerged after the Korean War are reflective of the divergent paths each region took in terms of economic development, political ideologies, and external influences. The consequences of these disparities continue to shape the lives of people living on the Korean Peninsula, underscoring the enduring impact of the Korean War on history and the need for further understanding and analysis by historians.

The Ideological Divide

The Korean War was not simply a military conflict between North and South Korea; it was a clash of ideologies that had far-reaching consequences. This subchapter will delve into the ideological divide that fueled the war and explore its enduring impact on history.

At its core, the Korean War was a manifestation of the broader ideological struggle between communism and democracy during the Cold War era. The war was a direct result of the ideological divide between the Soviet Union, which supported the communist regime in North Korea, and the United States, which backed the democratic government in the South. This clash of ideologies would shape the course of the conflict and have lasting implications for the Korean Peninsula and the world.

The role of propaganda in the Korean War cannot be overlooked. Both sides utilized propaganda to shape public opinion and rally support for their cause. This subchapter will explore the various propaganda campaigns employed by the North and South, examining how they influenced public perception and contributed to the ideological divide between the two sides.

The impact of the Korean War on the division of the Korean Peninsula cannot be understated. The war resulted in the establishment of the Demilitarized Zone (DMZ), which has served as a physical reminder of the ideological and geopolitical divide between North and South Korea. This subchapter will delve into the long-lasting consequences of this division, including the strained relations between the two countries and the ongoing threat of conflict.

External powers also played a significant role in the Korean War, further exacerbating the ideological divide. The involvement of countries like the United States, China, and the Soviet Union not only heightened the intensity of the conflict but also shaped its outcome. This subchapter will analyze the influence of these external powers and their impact on the ideological struggle in Korea.

Additionally, this subchapter will explore the experiences of Korean prisoners of war (POWs) during and after the war. Many POWs faced brutal treatment and endured harsh conditions, further deepening the ideological divide between the two sides. The subchapter will also examine the cultural and societal changes that took place in North and South Korea post-war, highlighting how the conflict influenced the development of each country.

Furthermore, the role of women in the Korean War will be explored, shedding light on their contributions to the conflict and the challenges they faced. The subchapter will also discuss the legacy of the Korean War on international relations and geopolitics, examining how the war shaped alliances and power dynamics in the region.

Lastly, the economic consequences of the Korean War will be examined, including the impact on trade, infrastructure, and development. The subchapter will also address the role of the United Nations in the Korean War and the human rights violations that occurred during the conflict, highlighting the need for accountability and justice.

In summary, this subchapter on the ideological divide in the Korean War will provide historians with a comprehensive understanding of the conflict's enduring impact on history. By examining various aspects such as propaganda, external powers, POW experiences, societal changes, and economic consequences, it will shed light on how the war shaped the Korean Peninsula and influenced international relations.

Reunification Efforts and Challenges

The Korean War, often referred to as the "Forgotten Conflict," has had an enduring impact on history. As historians, it is crucial to examine the reunification efforts and challenges that have shaped the Korean Peninsula since the war's end.

Following the armistice in 1953, Korea remained deeply divided, with the Demilitarized Zone (DMZ) acting as a physical and symbolic representation of the ongoing division. Reunification became a common aspiration for both North and South Korea, but the challenges were immense.

One of the primary obstacles to reunification was the role of propaganda during the war. Both sides heavily employed propaganda techniques to manipulate public opinion and justify their actions. This created deep-seated mistrust and animosity between the two Koreas, making the path towards reunification even more challenging.

External powers also played a significant role in the Korean War and subsequent reunification efforts. The influence of the United States, China, and the Soviet Union greatly impacted the conflict's outcome and further complicated the reunification process. These external powers had their own geopolitical interests, often at odds with the aspirations of the Korean people.

The experiences of Korean prisoners of war (POWs) during and after the war also shed light on the challenges of reunification. Many POWs faced immense physical and psychological trauma, and their experiences shaped their views on reunification. Some embraced the idea, while others harbored deep resentment and distrust.

The cultural and societal changes in North and South Korea post-war further complicated reunification. The two countries developed distinct identities and systems, with North Korea embracing a totalitarian regime and South Korea adopting a democratic framework. These differences created significant barriers to reunification, as both sides struggled to find common ground.

The role of women in the Korean War and subsequent reunification efforts cannot be overlooked. Women played a crucial role in supporting the war effort and rebuilding their communities after the conflict. Their contributions and voices have been instrumental in shaping the dialogue around reunification and challenging traditional gender roles.

The legacy of the Korean War on international relations and geopolitics cannot be underestimated. The war highlighted the tensions between the United States and the Soviet Union, leading to a prolonged period of Cold War rivalry. The ongoing division on the Korean Peninsula has also been a constant source of tension in the region, impacting diplomatic relations and regional stability.

Economically, the Korean War had profound consequences. Both North and South Korea faced severe devastation, with infrastructure and industries destroyed. Reunification efforts would require significant investment and restructuring to bridge the economic disparities between the two Koreas.

Furthermore, the United Nations' role in the Korean War and subsequent reunification efforts shaped the international community's response to conflict and the promotion of human rights. The atrocities committed during the war, including human rights violations, have been a focus of investigation and accountability.

In conclusion, the reunification of the Korean Peninsula has been a complex and challenging process. The enduring impact of the Korean War, the role of propaganda, external powers, POW experiences, cultural changes, women's contributions, and the economic and human rights consequences have all shaped the narrative and obstacles of reunification. As historians, it is vital to explore these aspects to better understand the lingering effects of the Korean War and the ongoing pursuit of reunification.

Chapter 4: The Influence of External Powers in the Korean War

United States' Involvement

The United States' involvement in the Korean War was significant and had a lasting impact on both the war itself and the subsequent history of the Korean Peninsula. As one of the major external powers in the conflict, the United States played a crucial role in shaping the outcome of the war and its aftermath.

From the outset, the United States saw the Korean War as a crucial battleground in the larger context of the Cold War between the United States and the Soviet Union. The United States, under the leadership of President Harry S. Truman, viewed North Korea's invasion of South Korea as an act of communist aggression and a threat to the stability of the region. In response, the United States quickly mobilized its military forces and intervened in the conflict to support South Korea.

The United States' involvement in the Korean War was not limited to military support. The United States also played a key role in shaping the narrative of the war through propaganda. The US government used various media outlets to portray the war as a fight against communism, highlighting the alleged atrocities committed by North Korean and Chinese forces. This propaganda campaign aimed to garner public support for the war effort and maintain the United States' image as the defender of democracy.

Furthermore, the United States' involvement in the Korean War had a profound impact on the Korean Peninsula's division. The war ultimately ended in a stalemate, with the creation of the demilitarized zone (DMZ) along the 38th parallel, which continues to divide North and South Korea to this day. The United States' role in maintaining the DMZ and providing military support to South Korea has contributed to the long-lasting division and tense relations between the two countries.

The experiences of Korean prisoners of war (POWs) during and after the war were also influenced by the United States' involvement. The United States held thousands of North Korean and Chinese POWs in prisoner-of-war camps, where they faced harsh conditions and mistreatment. The United States' treatment of POWs during the war and its handling of repatriation after the armistice are subjects of ongoing debate and controversy.

In addition, the United States' involvement in the Korean War brought about cultural and societal changes in both North and South Korea. The war disrupted traditional Korean society and led to the displacement of millions of people. In South Korea, the war led to a rapid industrialization and modernization, while in North Korea, it reinforced the cult of personality around leader Kim Il-sung.

The legacy of the Korean War on international relations and geopolitics cannot be understated. The war marked the first major military conflict of the Cold War and set the stage for future conflicts in Asia, including the Vietnam War. It also demonstrated the United States' commitment to containing communism and solidified its role as a global superpower.

Furthermore, the economic consequences of the Korean War were significant. The war left both North and South Korea devastated, with massive infrastructure damage and a heavy loss of life. The United States provided significant financial aid to South Korea to aid in its recovery and development, further strengthening its influence in the region.

The role of the United Nations (UN) in the Korean War was another important aspect of the United States' involvement. The United States, along with other UN member states, supported South Korea under the UN flag, marking the first major military intervention by the international organization. The UN's involvement in the war highlighted the importance of collective security and the United States' commitment to the UN's principles.

Lastly, the Korean War saw numerous human rights violations committed by all sides involved in the conflict. The United States was not exempt from criticism, as reports of civilian casualties, indiscriminate bombings, and other atrocities emerged. These human rights violations continue to be investigated and addressed, highlighting the complex and often devastating consequences of war.

In conclusion, the United States' involvement in the Korean War had a profound and enduring impact on history. From shaping the outcome of the war to influencing the division of the Korean Peninsula, the United States played a crucial role in the conflict. The cultural, societal, and economic changes that occurred as a result of the war, as well as the legacy it left on international relations and human rights, continue to shape the Korean Peninsula and the world at large.

Soviet Union's Role

The Soviet Union played a significant role in the Korean War, which had far-reaching consequences for the Korean Peninsula and the global stage. As historians, it is crucial to understand the actions and motivations of the Soviet Union during this conflict in order to comprehend its enduring impact on history.

From the outset, the Soviet Union provided crucial support to North Korea, both militarily and politically. Soviet leader Joseph Stalin saw an opportunity to expand the influence of communism in Asia and to counter the United States' presence in the region. The Soviet Union supplied North Korea with weapons, ammunition, and military advisors, enabling the North Korean forces to launch a surprise attack on South Korea in June 1950.

Furthermore, the Soviet Union played a vital role in the United Nations Security Council during the early stages of the war. By boycotting the council in protest against the exclusion of the People's Republic of China, the Soviet Union allowed the UN to pass a resolution authorizing military intervention in Korea. This led to the formation of a UN-commanded multinational force, which included Soviet-allied countries like China and the Soviet Union's own troops.

However, the Soviet Union's involvement in the Korean War was not limited to military support. It also played a crucial role in the propaganda war. The Soviet Union utilized its media and propaganda machinery to shape the narrative of the conflict, painting the United States as an aggressor and portraying North Korea as the victim of imperialist aggression. This propaganda campaign aimed to rally support for North Korea and communism globally, especially in the so-called "Third World" countries.

Moreover, the Soviet Union's role in the Korean War had a lasting impact on the division of the Korean Peninsula. Under Soviet influence, the armistice agreement signed in 1953 established a demilitarized zone along the 38th parallel, effectively dividing Korea into North and South. This division, which still persists today, has had profound consequences for the Korean people, their societies, and the global geopolitical landscape.

In conclusion, the Soviet Union's role in the Korean War cannot be understated. From military support to propaganda campaigns and the division of the Korean Peninsula, the Soviet Union's actions had a lasting impact on the course and aftermath of the war. Understanding this role is essential for historians studying the Korean War and its enduring impact on history, international relations, and human rights.

China's Intervention

The Korean War is often remembered as a conflict primarily between North and South Korea, but it would be remiss to overlook the significant role played by China. In this subchapter, we delve into China's intervention in the Korean War and its enduring impact on history.

China's entry into the war in 1950 marked a turning point in the conflict. As the North Korean forces faced setbacks against the South Korean and United Nations (UN) troops, China saw an opportunity to assert its influence and protect its own interests. Historians have debated the motivations behind China's intervention, ranging from ideological solidarity with fellow communist nations to fears of a Western presence on its doorstep.

The Chinese People's Volunteer Army (PVA) launched a massive offensive against the UN forces, pushing them back and retaking much of the territory that had been lost. The intervention not only changed the course of the war but also escalated its scale and intensity. The conflict transformed from a civil war into a proxy war between the United States and its allies, and China and the Soviet Union.

China's intervention had a profound impact on the Korean Peninsula's division. The PVA's successful push southwards led to a stalemate and the establishment of the demilitarized zone (DMZ), which remains to this day. The division of Korea became entrenched, and efforts to reunify the peninsula have been elusive ever since.

Furthermore, China's intervention highlighted the influence of external powers in the Korean War. The conflict became a battleground for Cold War rivalries, with the United States supporting South Korea and China and the Soviet Union backing North Korea. This external involvement not only prolonged the war but also raised the stakes and the potential for a wider conflagration.

China's intervention also had a profound impact on the experiences of Korean prisoners of war (POWs). Thousands of South Korean soldiers were captured by the Chinese and subjected to harsh treatment, including forced labor and indoctrination. Even after the war's end, many POWs faced difficulties reintegrating into society and suffered from physical and psychological traumas.

In conclusion, China's intervention in the Korean War had a far-reaching impact on various aspects, from the division of the Korean Peninsula to the experiences of POWs. Understanding China's role is crucial for historians seeking to comprehend the complexities and enduring legacies of the Korean War.

Other International Players and their Impact

Throughout the course of the Korean War, various international players had a significant impact on the conflict and its aftermath. These players, though often overshadowed by the United States and the Soviet Union, played crucial roles in shaping the outcome of the war and its enduring impact on history.

One such international player was China. As the war escalated, China, under the leadership of Mao Zedong, intervened on behalf of North Korea. This intervention not only provided critical military support to the North Korean forces but also escalated the scale and intensity of the conflict. China's involvement transformed the Korean War from a regional conflict to an international proxy war, further heightening tensions between the United States and the Soviet Union.

Another important player in the Korean War was Japan. Despite being stripped of its colonial holdings in Korea following World War II, Japan still maintained a significant economic influence on the Korean Peninsula. Japanese companies, eager to exploit the war-driven economic opportunities, became major suppliers of goods and services to both

North and South Korea. This economic involvement had far-reaching consequences, shaping the post-war economic development of both countries and laying the groundwork for the economic powerhouses they would become in subsequent decades.

Additionally, the United Nations played a crucial role in the Korean War. The UN, led by the United States, intervened in the conflict under the banner of promoting international peace and security. This marked the first time the UN had authorized the use of military force to counter aggression, setting an important precedent for future international interventions. The UN's involvement also had a lasting impact on the Korean Peninsula, as it led to the establishment of the demilitarized zone (DMZ) and the division of Korea into North and South.

Furthermore, the Soviet Union, although primarily involved through its support for North Korea, played a significant role in the Korean War. Soviet military aid, including the supply of weapons and equipment, bolstered North Korean forces, making them a formidable opponent for the United Nations and South Korean forces. The Soviet Union's involvement also highlighted the global ideological struggle between communism and capitalism, further fueling Cold War tensions.

In conclusion, the Korean War was not simply a conflict between North and South Korea. It involved a complex web of international players, each with their own motivations and interests. China, Japan, the United Nations, and the Soviet Union, among others, shaped the course and outcome of the war, leaving a lasting impact on the Korean Peninsula and the wider world. Understanding the roles and impacts of these international players is crucial to comprehending the enduring significance of the Korean War in history.

Chapter 5: The Experiences of Korean POWs during and after the War

POW Conditions during the War

During the Korean War, the conditions experienced by prisoners of war (POWs) were harsh and often deplorable. This subchapter delves into the various aspects of POW life, providing insights into the treatment, living conditions, and long-term consequences endured by these individuals.

The Korean War was marked by intense fighting, resulting in a large number of captured soldiers from both sides. However, the treatment of POWs differed significantly depending on which side held them. The North Korean and Chinese forces were notorious for subjecting their captives to brutal living conditions, physical and psychological torture, and forced labor. The POWs were often malnourished, living in squalid and overcrowded camps, with inadequate medical care. Interrogations aimed at extracting military intelligence were common, and those who resisted were subject to severe punishment, including beatings and even execution.

In contrast, the United Nations forces generally adhered to the standards set by the Geneva Conventions, providing better treatment to captured enemy soldiers. However, even under these conditions, POWs faced significant challenges. They often endured long marches to internment camps, lacking proper food, water, and shelter. Many suffered from illnesses and injuries sustained during combat, exacerbated by the difficult living conditions. The psychological toll was also immense, as the uncertainty of their fate weighed heavily on their minds.

The experiences of Korean POWs were particularly complex. Many were forcibly conscripted by both sides, with North Korean POWs facing the risk of being labeled "traitors" upon their return. These individuals often faced severe discrimination and social ostracism, as their loyalty was questioned by both North and South Koreans. South Korean POWs, on the other hand, were often hailed as heroes upon their release, but the trauma they endured during captivity left lasting scars on their physical and mental health.

The end of the war did not mark the end of suffering for many POWs. The repatriation process was prolonged, with some individuals held captive for years after the armistice was signed. Upon their release, many struggled to reintegrate into society, facing economic hardships and psychological trauma. Governments and international organizations attempted to provide support, but the magnitude of the issue meant that many POWs did not receive adequate assistance.

Understanding the conditions experienced by POWs during the Korean War is crucial to comprehending the broader impact of the conflict. The mistreatment of POWs not only violated human rights but also had long-lasting consequences on the individuals involved and the societies they returned to. The experiences of POWs serve as a stark reminder of the horrors of war and the importance of upholding humanitarian principles even in times of conflict.

Treatment of POWs by Different Parties

The treatment of prisoners of war (POWs) during the Korean War varied significantly among the different parties involved in the conflict. This subchapter explores the contrasting experiences of POWs from various perspectives, shedding light on the human rights violations that occurred during this tumultuous period.

The Korean War was marked by intense brutality, with both the North Korean and Chinese forces exhibiting harsh treatment towards captured United Nations (UN) soldiers. Many POWs endured physical abuse, malnutrition, and forced labor under appalling conditions. The Chinese

Communist forces, in particular, implemented a strategy of "reeducation" aimed at indoctrinating and brainwashing prisoners to embrace communist ideology. This involved psychological manipulation, coercion, and even torture. Such treatment resulted in long-lasting emotional and psychological trauma for many POWs.

Conversely, the treatment of North Korean and Chinese POWs by the UN forces was generally more in line with the principles of the Geneva Conventions. While this does not absolve all instances of mistreatment or abuse, the overall approach was more humane. The UN forces provided basic necessities such as food, shelter, and medical care to the captured enemy combatants. Many POWs from North Korea and China opted to defect to the South or other UN countries due to the stark contrast in treatment.

The experiences of South Korean POWs were particularly complex. Those captured by North Korean and Chinese forces faced the same harsh conditions as their UN counterparts. However, upon repatriation, some South Korean POWs were treated as traitors by their own government due to suspicions of collaboration with the enemy. This resulted in further mistreatment, imprisonment, and even execution in some cases. The discrimination and stigma attached to these former POWs persisted long after the war ended, leading to significant societal and cultural changes in South Korea.

The treatment of POWs during the Korean War had a lasting impact on international relations and human rights. The egregious human rights violations committed by the North Korean and Chinese forces brought global attention to the need for greater protections for POWs. This led to reforms in international law and the strengthening of the Geneva Conventions to ensure the proper treatment and rights of captured soldiers in future conflicts.

In conclusion, the treatment of POWs during the Korean War varied significantly depending on the party involved. While the UN forces generally adhered to international standards, the North Korean and Chinese forces subjected POWs to severe mistreatment and indoctrination. The experiences of POWs during and after the war highlight the importance of addressing human rights violations and the enduring impact of the conflict on history.

Repatriation and its Challenges

The repatriation of prisoners of war (POWs) during and after the Korean War posed significant challenges for all parties involved. This subchapter explores the complexities and difficulties faced by the nations involved in repatriating their soldiers, shedding light on the enduring impact of this process.

The repatriation process was marred by political, cultural, and humanitarian challenges. The Korean War, often referred to as "The War That Has not Ended," left a lasting divide on the Korean Peninsula. As a result, the repatriation of POWs became entangled in the wider political struggle between North and South Korea. Both sides used repatriation as a means of propaganda, attempting to showcase their own political system as superior. This highlights the role of propaganda in the Korean War and its influence on repatriation efforts.

External powers also played a significant role in the repatriation process. The Soviet Union and the United States, as the main actors in the conflict, exerted their influence to ensure the return of their POWs. This further complicated repatriation efforts, as the interests of external powers were often at odds with those of the Korean people.

The experiences of Korean POWs during and after the war were particularly challenging. Many faced interrogation, torture, and indoctrination, making the decision to return home a difficult one. The cultural and societal changes that occurred in North and South Korea post-war further added to the challenges faced by the repatriated POWs.

The role of women in the Korean War and its impact on repatriation efforts cannot be overlooked. Women played various roles during the conflict, including nurses, soldiers, and spies. Their experiences and contributions influenced the repatriation process, as they too faced the challenges of returning to a divided Korea.

The legacy of the Korean War on international relations and geopolitics had a significant impact on repatriation efforts. The war heightened tensions between the United States and the Soviet Union, leading to a global power struggle that affected the repatriation process and prolonged the suffering of POWs.

Furthermore, the economic consequences of the Korean War further complicated repatriation efforts. The war had devastating effects on the Korean economy, making the return and reintegration of POWs a challenging task for both North and South Korea.

Finally, the human rights violations that occurred during the Korean War had a profound impact on the repatriation process. Many POWs were subject to abuse and mistreatment, further complicating their return and reintegration into society.

In conclusion, the repatriation of POWs during and after the Korean War was fraught with challenges. Political, cultural, and humanitarian factors, as well as the influence of external powers, played a significant role in shaping the repatriation process. The experiences of Korean POWs, the role of women, the legacy on international relations, and the economic consequences of the war all contributed to the complexities faced by those involved. Understanding these challenges is crucial to comprehending the enduring impact of the Korean War on history.

Long-term Psychological and Physical Effects

The Korean War, often referred to as the "Forgotten Conflict," may have ended over six decades ago, but its impact on history and the individuals involved remains enduring. This subchapter delves into the long-term psychological and physical effects that the war has had on those directly affected by it.

The Korean War was a brutal and intense conflict that left a lasting mark on the mental and physical well-being of soldiers and civilians alike. Soldiers who experienced the horrors of battle often suffered from post-traumatic stress disorder (PTSD) long after the war had ended. Flashbacks, nightmares, and severe anxiety plagued them, leading to difficulties in readjusting to civilian life. The psychological scars of the war remained a silent burden for many, affecting their relationships, careers, and overall quality of life.

Furthermore, the physical toll of the war cannot be underestimated. Many soldiers returned home with life-altering injuries, such as amputations, disabilities, and severe burns. These physical disabilities not only impacted their ability to engage in regular activities but also hindered their chances of securing employment and achieving financial stability.

Beyond the soldiers, the civilian population also experienced long-lasting psychological and physical effects. The constant shelling, displacement, and loss of loved ones resulted in widespread trauma for Korean civilians. The emotional scars endured, leading to higher rates of depression, anxiety, and other mental health disorders.

Moreover, the war had a significant impact on the Korean Peninsula's division, with families separated and a deep sense of loss instilled in communities. The division perpetuated a sense of mistrust and animosity, further exacerbating the psychological impact on the population.

To add to this, the war was not only fought on the battlefield but also through propaganda, which played a crucial role in shaping public opinion and manipulating emotions. This psychological warfare had a lasting impact on both North and South Korea, perpetuating the division and contributing to the ongoing tensions between the two nations.

In conclusion, the long-term psychological and physical effects of the Korean War have left an indelible mark on the individuals and communities involved. The trauma endured by soldiers, civilians, and the Korean Peninsula as a whole continues to shape their lives and the ongoing narrative of the war. Understanding these effects is crucial for historians studying the Korean War's enduring impact on history and its influence on various aspects, including international relations, human rights, and geopolitics.

Chapter 6: Cultural and Societal Changes in North and South Korea Post-War

North Korea's Juche Ideology

The Korean War had far-reaching consequences that continue to shape history, and one of the most intriguing aspects is the development and implementation of North Korea's Juche ideology. Juche, meaning "self-reliance," emerged as the guiding principle of North Korean society under the leadership of Kim Il-sung. This subchapter explores the origins, principles, and impact of Juche ideology on various aspects of Korean society during and after the Korean War.

Juche ideology was born out of the Korean War, a conflict that devastated the entire peninsula and left a lasting impact on both North and South Korea. It aimed to establish North Korea as a self-reliant socialist state, free from external influences and dependency. Juche emphasized the importance of national sovereignty and self-determination, rejecting any form of foreign intervention or dominance. This ideology became the cornerstone of North Korea's political, economic, and social systems.

In the context of the Korean War, Juche ideology played a significant role in shaping North Korea's resistance against the United States and its allies. Propaganda, another crucial element in the war, was used to promote the ideals of Juche and rally the North Korean people behind their leader. The role of propaganda in the Korean War is explored in detail in a separate chapter, but its influence on the promotion of Juche cannot be overlooked.

The impact of Juche ideology extended beyond the conflict itself. It influenced the division of the Korean Peninsula, as North Korea sought to establish its independent socialist state while South Korea aligned itself with the United States. The cultural and societal changes in both North and South Korea post-war were heavily influenced by Juche ideology, leading to contrasting systems and beliefs.

Juche ideology also impacted various aspects of North Korean society, including the role of women, the treatment of Korean POWs, and human rights violations during and after the war. The experiences of Korean POWs and the violation of human rights are particularly significant areas of study for historians. The legacy of the Korean War on international relations and geopolitics, as well as the economic consequences of the conflict, cannot be understood fully without considering the influence of Juche ideology.

This subchapter provides a comprehensive analysis of North Korea's Juche ideology, exploring its origins, principles, and impact on various aspects of Korean society. By understanding the ideological underpinnings of North Korea, historians can gain valuable insights into the complexities of the Korean War and its enduring impact on history.

South Korea's Economic Miracle

Subchapter: South Korea's Economic Miracle

Introduction:

The Korean War profoundly impacted the Korean Peninsula, leaving it devastated and divided. However, amidst the chaos and destruction, South Korea emerged as a remarkable success story, achieving what is often referred to as the "South Korean Economic Miracle." This subchapter explores the economic consequences of the Korean War and sheds light on South Korea's extraordinary transformation into a global economic powerhouse.

The Aftermath of War:

At the end of the Korean War in 1953, South Korea faced immense challenges. Its infrastructure was in ruins, its economy shattered, and its population scarred by years of conflict. Yet, against all odds, South Korea managed to rise from the ashes and embark on a path of rapid economic growth.

The Role of Government:

One crucial factor behind South Korea's economic miracle was the government's proactive and strategic approach. It implemented a series of policies aimed at fostering industrialization, export-led growth, and technological advancement. The government's strong intervention in the economy, coupled with policies encouraging entrepreneurship and innovation, played a pivotal role in South Korea's economic transformation.

The Chaebols and Industrialization:

The rise of the chaebols, large family-owned conglomerates, such as Samsung, Hyundai, and LG, played a significant role in South Korea's economic success. These conglomerates received government support and played a critical role in driving industrialization, contributing to the nation's export-oriented economy.

Investment in Education and Human Capital:

South Korea recognized the importance of investing in education and human capital to fuel economic growth. The government implemented policies that prioritized education, resulting in a highly skilled and educated workforce. This emphasis on education became a driving force behind South Korea's technological advancements and innovation.

Export-Oriented Economy:

South Korea adopted an export-oriented strategy, focusing on manufacturing industries such as automobiles, electronics, and shipbuilding. By leveraging its competitive advantage in labor-intensive industries and being open to foreign investment, South Korea became a global manufacturing hub and a leading exporter.

The Role of International Aid and Trade:

International aid and trade played a vital role in South Korea's economic development. The country received significant financial assistance from the United States and international organizations, which helped rebuild its infrastructure and stimulate economic growth. Additionally, South Korea actively engaged in international trade, establishing trade agreements and partnerships with various countries, further bolstering its economic growth.

Conclusion:

South Korea's economic miracle serves as a testament to the nation's resilience and determination. From a war-torn country, it transformed into one of the world's largest economies within a few decades. South Korea's success was fueled by government intervention, investment in education, export-oriented policies, and international aid and trade. The economic consequences of the Korean War, while initially devastating, ultimately paved the way for South Korea's remarkable rise on the world stage, leaving a lasting impact on global economic relations.

Social Reforms and Modernization

The Korean War not only left a lasting impact on the political and military landscape of the Korean Peninsula but also triggered significant social reforms and modernization in both North and South Korea. This subchapter delves into the transformative changes that occurred in various aspects of society after the war, shedding light on the long-term consequences of this conflict.

In the aftermath of the Korean War, both North and South Korea embarked on ambitious social reforms aimed at modernizing their societies. These reforms encompassed areas such as education, healthcare, and infrastructure development. The devastation caused by the war served as a catalyst for change, compelling the governments to invest heavily in rebuilding their societies and improving the living standards of their populations.

Education emerged as a key focus for social reform in post-war Korea. Governments in both North and South Korea recognized the importance of education in nation-building and initiated efforts to expand access to education for all citizens. Schools were built, curricula were revised, and literacy campaigns were launched to promote widespread education. These reforms played a crucial role in shaping the future generations and fostering a sense of national identity.

Furthermore, the Korean War brought about significant changes in gender roles and the role of women in society. With a large number of men being conscripted or killed during the war, women were forced to take on new responsibilities and contribute to the workforce. This shift in gender dynamics challenged traditional norms and paved the way for greater gender equality in post-war Korea.

In addition to social reforms, the Korean War also accelerated the process of modernization in terms of infrastructure development. Both North and South Korea invested heavily in rebuilding their war-torn cities and improving transportation networks. This modernization drive not only enhanced the overall quality of life but also laid the foundation for economic growth in the years to come.

Overall, the social reforms and modernization efforts that followed the Korean War had a profound and lasting impact on Korean society. These changes not only shaped the development trajectory of both North and South Korea but also influenced their respective political systems, economic structures, and cultural landscapes. By understanding the social reforms and modernization that occurred after the war, historians can gain a deeper insight into the long-term consequences of the Korean War and its enduring impact on history.

Impact on Cultural Identity

The Korean War, often referred to as "The Forgotten Conflict," had a profound impact on the cultural identity of both North and South Korea. This subchapter will delve into the various ways in which the war shaped and transformed the cultural landscape of the Korean Peninsula.

One of the most significant impacts of the Korean War on cultural identity was the division of the country into North and South Korea. The division not only created a physical separation between the two regions but also led to the emergence of distinct political ideologies and systems. North Korea adopted a communist regime under the leadership of Kim Il-sung, while South Korea embraced a capitalist democracy. These ideological differences had far-reaching consequences for the cultural development of both countries.

Propaganda played a pivotal role in shaping the cultural identity during the Korean War. Both sides engaged in extensive propaganda campaigns to rally support for their respective causes. This led to the dissemination of propaganda through various mediums, such as newspapers, radio, and even art. The war became a battle not only on the battlefield but also in the realm of public opinion, further fueling the divide between North and South Korea.

The experiences of Korean prisoners of war (POWs) during and after the war also had a profound impact on cultural identity. Many POWs faced brutal treatment and were subjected to intense indoctrination by their captors. Some even chose to defect to the opposing side, further complicating the issue of cultural identity and loyalty.

The cultural and societal changes that occurred in both North and South Korea post-war cannot be understated. In North Korea, the regime enforced strict control over cultural expression, promoting a state-sponsored ideology. On the other hand, South Korea experienced rapid economic growth and embraced Western influence, leading to the emergence of a vibrant pop culture industry.

The role of women in the Korean War also had a lasting impact on cultural identity. Women played significant roles as nurses, factory workers, and even combatants during the conflict. Their contributions challenged traditional gender roles and paved the way for greater gender equality in post-war Korean society.

The legacy of the Korean War on international relations and geopolitics cannot be ignored either. The war heightened tensions between the United States and the Soviet Union, setting the stage for the Cold War. It also solidified the division between communist and non-communist countries, shaping the global political landscape for decades to come.

In conclusion, the Korean War had a profound and lasting impact on the cultural identity of both North and South Korea. The division of the country, the role of propaganda, the experiences of POWs, and the cultural and societal changes that followed the war all contributed to shaping the unique cultural identities that exist in the Korean Peninsula today. Understanding these impacts is crucial in comprehending the enduring significance of the Korean War in history.

Chapter 7: The Role of Women in the Korean War

Women in Combat

The Korean War, often referred to as "The Forgotten Conflict," was a pivotal moment in history that had far-reaching impacts on various aspects of society. One area that is often overlooked is the role of women in combat during this war. Historians have typically focused on the geopolitical and military aspects of the conflict, but it is crucial to examine the experiences and contributions of women who served on the front lines.

Despite the traditional gender roles of the time, the Korean War witnessed an unprecedented number of women actively participating in combat. These women defied societal norms and proved that they were just as capable as their male counterparts. They served in a variety of roles, including nurses, medics, and even combat soldiers. Their sacrifices and bravery played a significant role in the overall war effort.

Propaganda also played a crucial role in shaping the perception of women's involvement in combat during the Korean War. Both the North and South Korean governments utilized propaganda to portray women as strong, patriotic, and dedicated soldiers. These images were meant to inspire and motivate the troops, as well as to rally support from the civilian population. The impact of this propaganda on public opinion cannot be understated.

The experiences of women serving in combat during the Korean War were undoubtedly challenging and often overlooked. Many faced discrimination and prejudice from their male counterparts, who questioned their abilities and undermined their contributions. Despite these obstacles, women soldiers demonstrated their skills and dedication, earning the respect of their fellow soldiers and commanders.

The legacy of women in combat during the Korean War extends beyond the immediate conflict. Their bravery and determination paved the way for future generations of women in the military. Their experiences challenged traditional gender roles and contributed to the ongoing fight for gender equality in the armed forces.

In conclusion, the role of women in combat during the Korean War is a significant aspect that deserves recognition and further exploration. Their contributions challenged gender norms, and their experiences provide valuable insights into the complexities of war. By examining their stories, we gain a more comprehensive understanding of the Korean War's enduring impact on history.

Women in Support Roles

Subchapter: Women in Support Roles

Throughout history, women have played significant but often overlooked roles in times of conflict and war. The Korean War was no exception, as women took on various support roles that were instrumental in the success and survival of their respective nations. This subchapter will shed light on the important contributions made by women during the Korean War, highlighting the roles they played in the realms of propaganda, nursing, intelligence, and more.

Propaganda, a powerful tool during times of war, saw the active participation of women in both North and South Korea. Women in the North were often tasked with disseminating propaganda messages to both the domestic and international audiences. Meanwhile, in the South, women played a vital role in producing and distributing pamphlets and flyers aimed at boosting morale and garnering support for the cause.

In the medical field, women made significant contributions as nurses, providing care and aid to injured soldiers on the front lines. Their bravery and dedication were evident as they worked tirelessly to save lives and alleviate suffering amidst the chaos of war. Furthermore, some women served as intelligence agents, relaying crucial information to their respective forces. Their efforts often went unnoticed due to the secretive nature of their work, but their contributions were invaluable to the war effort.

Beyond these specific roles, women in both North and South Korea experienced significant societal changes during and after the war. With many men away at the front, women took on more responsibilities in the workforce, contributing to the economic and industrial development of their nations. These changes challenged traditional gender roles and paved the way for the gradual empowerment of women in both North and South Korean societies.

Despite their contributions, the role of women in the Korean War has been largely neglected in historical narratives. Recognizing their efforts not only helps to paint a more accurate picture of the conflict but also highlights the importance of gender perspectives in understanding war and its lasting impact. By acknowledging the multifaceted roles women played in support positions, historians can provide a more comprehensive understanding of the Korean War and its enduring influence on history.

In conclusion, women played vital roles in support positions during the Korean War. From their involvement in propaganda to their contributions in nursing and intelligence, women made significant and often overlooked contributions to the war effort. By shining a light on the experiences and contributions of women during this conflict, historians can provide a more complete understanding of the Korean War's impact on history.

Women's Activism and Post-War Contributions

In the tumultuous aftermath of the Korean War, women played a vital role in rebuilding their shattered societies and advocating for change. Despite the patriarchal norms prevalent in the post-war era, women's activism emerged as a potent force, leaving an indelible mark on the Korean Peninsula's history.

Women's contributions to the post-war reconstruction efforts were multifaceted and far-reaching. In the economic sphere, women actively participated in rebuilding the war-torn economies of North and South Korea. They joined the labor force in large numbers, taking up roles in factories, farms, and various industries. By contributing to the economic recovery, they helped alleviate the devastating consequences of the war and paved the way for future development.

Moreover, women's activism extended beyond the economic realm. They played a crucial role in advocating for women's rights and gender equality. Recognizing the need for social change, women organized themselves into various groups and associations aimed at addressing the gender disparities prevalent in Korean society. Through these organizations, they voiced their concerns and demands, pushing for legal reforms and societal transformations. Their efforts led to significant advancements in areas such as education, employment, and political participation for women.

Women's activism also played a pivotal role in shaping the political landscape of post-war Korea. Many women actively participated in political movements and organizations, fighting for democracy and human rights. Their involvement was instrumental in challenging the authoritarian regimes that emerged after the war and demanding a more inclusive and egalitarian society. Their struggles and sacrifices paved the way for a more democratic Korea, where women's voices and rights are increasingly recognized and valued.

Moreover, women's activism was not limited to the Korean Peninsula. Korean women, both in the North and South, reached out to the international community to raise awareness about the Korean War's enduring impact and the human rights violations that occurred during and after the conflict. They formed alliances with women's organizations worldwide, amplifying their voices and advocating for justice and accountability.

The contributions of women in post-war Korea have left a lasting legacy. Their activism and resilience have shaped the society and politics of the Korean Peninsula, fostering greater equality and social progress. Today, women continue to play a pivotal role in Korean society, driving change and advocating for a more inclusive and just future.

In conclusion, women's activism and post-war contributions were instrumental in shaping the course of Korean history after the Korean War. Their economic, social, and political efforts were crucial in rebuilding the nation and advocating for gender equality and human rights. As historians, it is essential to recognize and celebrate the contributions of women in the Korean War and its aftermath, as they have played a pivotal role in shaping the world we live in today.

Gender Dynamics and Shifts in Society

The Korean War was not only a military conflict but also a catalyst for significant societal changes, particularly in terms of gender dynamics. This subchapter explores the role of women during the war and the subsequent cultural and societal shifts in both North and South Korea.

During the Korean War, women played a critical role in various capacities. While men were fighting on the front lines, women stepped into traditionally male-dominated roles, such as factories, farms, and hospitals. They became the backbone of the economy, ensuring the country's survival in the face of adversity. This marked a significant departure from traditional gender roles, challenging the societal norms of the time.

However, despite their invaluable contributions, women faced numerous challenges and discrimination during and after the war. Their roles were often downplayed or overlooked, and they were expected to return to their pre-war domestic roles once the conflict ended. This disparity between their wartime contributions and post-war expectations created tensions and fueled the need for societal change.

The cultural and societal changes in North and South Korea post-war were marked by a gradual shift towards gender equality. Women began increasingly participating in the workforce and pursuing education, challenging traditional gender norms. The war had exposed the capabilities and resilience of women, leading to a reevaluation of their roles in society.

In North Korea, the government actively promoted gender equality as part of its socialist ideology. Women were encouraged to work and contribute to the nation's development alongside men. This emphasis on gender equality was reflected in policies promoting women's education and employment opportunities.

In South Korea, societal changes were influenced by external powers, particularly the United States. The American presence brought with it new ideas and values, including the notion of gender equality. As South Korea embraced modernization and industrialization, women gained increased access to education and employment opportunities.

However, despite these positive changes, gender inequality still persisted in both North and South Korea. Women continued to face barriers and discrimination, albeit to varying degrees, hindering their full participation in society.

Understanding the gender dynamics and shifts in Korean society is crucial for comprehending the lasting impact of the Korean War. By examining the role of women during the conflict and the subsequent societal changes, historians can gain valuable insights into the complex legacy of the war and its ongoing influence on gender relations in Korea.

Chapter 8: The Legacy of the Korean War on International Relations and Geopolitics

Cold War Dynamics and the Korean War

The Korean War is often referred to as "the forgotten conflict," but its impact on history is enduring. Understanding the dynamics of the Cold War and how they influenced the Korean War is vital to comprehending the complexities of this often overlooked conflict.

The Korean War was a direct result of the Cold War tensions between the Soviet Union and the United States. The division of Korea into North and South after World War II, with the North falling under Soviet influence and the South under American control, set the stage for a proxy war between these two superpowers. The Korean War became a battleground for their ideological struggle, with the communist North seeking to unify the peninsula under its rule, while the capitalist South aimed to resist this aggression.

Propaganda played a significant role in the Korean War, with both sides utilizing it to shape public opinion and rally support for their cause. The North Korean regime, under Kim Il-sung, employed propaganda to promote the idea of a unified, socialist Korea, while the South Korean government, with the help of the United States, highlighted the threat of communism and the need to defend democracy.

The Korean War had a profound impact on the division of the Korean Peninsula. The war ended in an armistice, not a peace treaty, leaving the North and South technically still at war. This division has endured for over seven decades, resulting in two distinct societies with vastly different political systems and economic development.

External powers, particularly the Soviet Union and the United States, exerted significant influence in the Korean War. The Soviet Union provided military support to North Korea, while the United States led the United Nations forces in defense of South Korea. These external powers not only shaped the outcome of the war but also influenced the subsequent geopolitical landscape of the region.

The experiences of Korean prisoners of war (POWs) during and after the conflict were often harrowing. Many POWs faced brutal treatment, including physical and psychological torture. Even after the war, the repatriation process was challenging, with some prisoners forcefully sent back to their home countries against their will.

The cultural and societal changes in North and South Korea following the war were profound. North Korea embraced a strict communist ideology, limiting personal freedoms and promoting a cult of personality around its leaders. In contrast, South Korea underwent rapid economic development, transforming from a war-torn nation into an industrial powerhouse.

Women played a vital role in the Korean War, both on the front lines and in supporting roles. They served as nurses, interpreters, and guerrilla fighters, contributing significantly to the war effort.

The legacy of the Korean War on international relations and geopolitics cannot be overstated. The conflict solidified the division between the communist and capitalist blocs and heightened tensions during the Cold War. It also reinforced the United States' commitment to containing communism and defending its allies in East Asia.

The economic consequences of the Korean War were substantial. The conflict caused widespread destruction, resulting in a significant loss of infrastructure and resources. However, South Korea's subsequent economic growth, known as the "Miracle on the Han River," defied all expectations and transformed the country into one of the world's leading economies.

The United Nations played a crucial role in the Korean War, with member states contributing troops and resources to the multinational force that defended South Korea. The conflict marked the first major test for the newly formed international organization and showcased its ability to address global security challenges.

Human rights violations during the Korean War were widespread. Both sides committed acts of violence against civilians, including massacres and forced displacements. The war left a lasting trauma on the Korean people, and unresolved human rights issues continue to impact the region.

In conclusion, understanding the Cold War dynamics and their influence on the Korean War is vital for historians to grasp the complexities of this forgotten conflict. The war's enduring impact on history, from the role of propaganda to the division of the Korean Peninsula, the influence of external powers, and the experiences of POWs, cannot be underestimated. The cultural, societal, and economic changes in North and South Korea post-war, as well as the role of women, the legacy on international relations, and the human rights violations during the conflict, all contribute to the significance of the Korean War in shaping not only the Korean Peninsula but also the global landscape.

Impact on East Asian Security

The Korean War, often referred to as the "Forgotten Conflict," had a significant impact on East Asian security. This subchapter explores the repercussions of the war on the region's stability, international relations, and geopolitical dynamics. As historians, it is crucial to understand the far-reaching consequences of this war, which continue to shape East Asian security to this day.

The Korean War: The War That Has not Ended

The division of Korea into North and South, resulting from the Korean War, has remained a contentious issue. The ongoing conflict and the absence of a formal peace treaty have contributed to a persistent state of tension and instability on the Korean Peninsula. This unresolved conflict has had a direct impact on East Asian security, as neighboring countries navigate the potential risks of a resurgent conflict.

The Influence of External Powers in the Korean War

The involvement of external powers, particularly the United States and China, had a profound impact on East Asian security during the Korean War. The conflict served as a proxy battleground for the broader Cold War between the Soviet Union and the United States, exacerbating regional tensions and heightening fears of a broader conflict in East Asia.

The Legacy of the Korean War on International Relations and Geopolitics

The Korean War significantly affected international relations and geopolitics in East Asia. The war solidified the divide between communist and non-communist states, leading to the further entrenchment of Cold War dynamics in the region. It also highlighted the importance of alliances and collective security arrangements, particularly with the involvement of the United Nations.

The Economic Consequences of the Korean War

The Korean War had a devastating impact on the economies of both North and South Korea. The destruction of infrastructure, loss of lives, and disruption to trade severely hindered economic development in the region. This economic setback had long-term consequences for East Asian security, as it contributed to the economic disparities between North and South Korea and influenced their respective political and military strategies.

In conclusion, the Korean War's impact on East Asian security cannot be underestimated. The ongoing division of the Korean Peninsula, the involvement of external powers, and the economic consequences of the war have all shaped the region's stability, international relations, and geopolitical dynamics. As historians, it is essential to delve into these issues to gain a comprehensive understanding of the enduring impact of the Korean War on East Asian security.

Lessons Learned and Future Conflict Prevention

Subchapter: Lessons Learned and Future Conflict Prevention

The Korean War, often referred to as the "Forgotten Conflict," has undoubtedly left an enduring impact on history. As historians, it is crucial to delve into the various facets of this war and analyze the lessons learned to prevent future conflicts of a similar magnitude. This subchapter aims to explore the insights gained from the Korean War and shed light on the path towards conflict prevention.

One of the most significant lessons learned from the Korean War is the role of propaganda in shaping public opinion and fueling tensions. The war was characterized by intense propaganda campaigns from both sides, highlighting the importance of understanding and countering such efforts in future conflicts. Historians must delve into the influence of propaganda on public perception and the implications it holds for conflict prevention.

Furthermore, the Korean War resulted in the division of the Korean Peninsula into North and South, which remains a geopolitical hotspot even today. By studying the impact of this division, historians can gain insight into the complexities of post-war territorial disputes and work towards preventing similar divisions in future conflicts.

External powers played a crucial role in the Korean War, with both the United States and the Soviet Union backing opposing sides. Analyzing the influence of external powers in the conflict can provide crucial lessons on the dangers of proxy wars and the importance of international diplomacy in preventing future conflicts.

The experiences of Korean prisoners of war (POWs) during and after the war also offer valuable insights. Understanding the treatment of POWs and the challenges they faced upon their release can guide efforts to ensure humane treatment and successful reintegration of prisoners in future conflicts.

The Korean War triggered significant cultural and societal changes in North and South Korea. Exploring the post-war developments can provide historians with a deeper understanding of the long-term consequences of conflict and the challenges faced by societies in rebuilding and reconciling.

The role of women in the Korean War is another aspect that warrants attention. By examining the contributions and experiences of women during the war, historians can shed light on the often overlooked roles and perspectives of women in conflicts and work towards a more inclusive understanding of war's impact.

The legacy of the Korean War on international relations and geopolitics cannot be overstated. Analyzing this legacy can help historians identify patterns and dynamics that may contribute to future conflicts, allowing for more informed policies and strategies.

Moreover, the economic consequences of the Korean War highlight the importance of understanding the interplay between conflict and economic stability. By exploring the economic ramifications of the war, historians can contribute to the development of strategies that promote economic resilience and prevent conflicts driven by economic disparities.

The role of the United Nations in the Korean War also deserves attention. Assessing the successes and failures of the UN's intervention can inform future efforts in conflict prevention and peacekeeping, emphasizing the importance of international cooperation and multilateral approaches.

Finally, the human rights violations during the Korean War underline the necessity of safeguarding human rights in times of conflict. By examining these violations, historians can advocate for the protection of human rights and contribute to the development of ethical frameworks for conflict resolution.

In conclusion, the lessons learned from the Korean War provide invaluable insights into conflict prevention and resolution. By delving into various aspects, such as propaganda, external powers, POW experiences, cultural changes, women's roles, economic consequences, and human rights violations, historians can contribute to a more comprehensive understanding of the war's enduring impact on history. Through this understanding, future conflicts can be prevented, and steps can be taken towards a more peaceful world.

The Korean War as a Precedent for Global Conflicts

The Korean War, often referred to as "The Forgotten Conflict," holds an enduring impact on history that extends far beyond the Korean Peninsula. This subchapter delves into the significance of this war as a precedent for future global conflicts, providing valuable insights for historians and scholars interested in understanding the broader implications of this often overshadowed conflict.

One of the key takeaways from the Korean War is the lasting impact of propaganda. Both sides, North and South Korea, as well as external powers such as the United States and the Soviet Union, heavily relied on propaganda to manipulate public opinion and rally support for their respective causes. This chapter explores the role of propaganda in shaping the narrative of the Korean War and its influence on subsequent conflicts.

Additionally, the Korean War serves as a stark reminder of the devastating consequences of external powers' involvement in regional conflicts. The influence of the United States and the Soviet Union in this war highlights the dangers of geopolitical rivalries and the potential for proxy wars, a phenomenon that would become all too common during the Cold War. Historians will find valuable insights into the dynamics of external powers' involvement in conflicts and its impact on international relations.

Furthermore, this subchapter delves into the experiences of Korean prisoners of war (POWs) during and after the conflict. Examining the treatment of POWs provides a lens through which historians can analyze the human rights violations that occurred during the Korean War and shed light on the broader issue of war crimes and violations of international humanitarian law.

The Korean War also sparked profound cultural and societal changes in both North and South Korea. By exploring these changes, historians gain a deeper understanding of the long-lasting ramifications of war on a society's cultural fabric and social structures.

This subchapter also delves into the economic consequences of the Korean War, focusing on the impact on both North and South Korea. By examining the economic aftermath of the conflict, historians can draw parallels to other post-war societies and gain insights into the challenges of rebuilding and recovering from a devastating conflict.

In conclusion, the Korean War serves as a crucial precedent for global conflicts, providing valuable lessons for historians and scholars interested in the long-term impact of regional conflicts on international relations, geopolitics, propaganda, human rights, culture, and economics. By delving into these various aspects, this subchapter offers a comprehensive analysis of the enduring legacy of the Korean War.

Chapter 9: The Economic Consequences of the Korean War

Destruction of Infrastructure and Industries

The Korean War was a devastating conflict that left a lasting impact on the Korean Peninsula and its people. One of the most significant consequences of the war was the widespread destruction of infrastructure and industries, which had far-reaching implications both during and after the conflict.

During the war, both North and South Korea witnessed the systematic targeting and destruction of vital infrastructure such as roads, bridges, railways, and power plants. This deliberate destruction was aimed at crippling the enemy's logistical capabilities and disrupting their ability to sustain military operations. As a result, both sides experienced severe disruptions in transportation, communication, and power supply, which further exacerbated the challenges faced by the combatants.

Industries, especially those involved in manufacturing and agriculture, were also heavily impacted by the war. Factories, mines, and farms were destroyed or severely damaged, leading to a significant decline in production and output. This not only hindered the war effort but also had long-term repercussions on the economic development of both North and South Korea.

The destruction of infrastructure and industries had a profound effect on the Korean Peninsula's division. With vital transportation links severed and industries in ruins, the division between the North and South became more pronounced. The lack of infrastructure made it difficult for people to move freely between the two regions, further deepening the political and social divide.

External powers played a crucial role in exacerbating the destruction of infrastructure and industries during the war. The involvement of major powers like the United States, China, and the Soviet Union provided the combatants with advanced weaponry and military support, which led to more extensive damage to critical infrastructure. Additionally, bombing campaigns by the United States caused significant destruction, particularly in North Korea.

The economic consequences of the war were severe and long-lasting. The destruction of industries and infrastructure hampered post-war reconstruction efforts, hindering economic recovery. Both North and South Korea faced immense challenges in rebuilding their economies and improving the living standards of their people.

In conclusion, the destruction of infrastructure and industries during the Korean War had profound and enduring consequences. It deepened the division of the Korean Peninsula, hindered economic development, and affected the lives of millions of people. Understanding the impact of this destruction is crucial for historians seeking to comprehend the long-term effects of the Korean War on the region and its people.

Economic Recovery and Development Efforts

The Korean War, often referred to as the "Forgotten Conflict," had a profound impact on history that continues to resonate to this day. While much attention has been given to the military and political aspects of the war, the economic consequences and subsequent recovery and development efforts are often overlooked. This subchapter aims to shed light on the economic aftermath of the Korean War and the efforts made towards recovery and development.

The Korean War left both North and South Korea devastated, with infrastructure in ruins, industries decimated, and a staggering loss of human capital. The division of the Korean Peninsula further exacerbated these challenges. In the years following the armistice, both sides faced the arduous task of rebuilding their economies and fostering development.

South Korea, with the support of the United States and other Western powers, embarked on an ambitious path towards recovery. The government implemented economic policies that focused on export-oriented industrialization, which proved to be immensely successful. The country's economy experienced rapid growth, transforming it into one of the world's leading economies today.

In contrast, North Korea pursued a different economic model, emphasizing self-reliance and central planning. However, the country faced numerous challenges, including a lack of resources, technological backwardness, and international isolation. Despite these obstacles, North Korea managed to make some progress, albeit at a slower pace compared to its southern counterpart.

The influence of external powers in the Korean War had a significant impact on the subsequent economic recovery. The United States, in particular, played a pivotal role in providing aid and investment to South Korea, helping to rebuild its infrastructure and industrial base. The legacy of this support can still be seen in the strong economic ties between the two countries today.

The economic consequences of the Korean War also had a profound effect on international relations and geopolitics. The war highlighted the importance of East Asia in the global economy and intensified the rivalry between the United States and the Soviet Union. It also led to the establishment of the United Nations Command and the United Nations Korean Reconstruction Agency, which played crucial roles in facilitating economic recovery efforts.

Furthermore, the experiences of Korean Prisoners of War (POWs) during and after the war had a lasting impact on the economic recovery.

Many POWs faced difficulties reintegrating into society and rebuilding their lives, which underscored the need for social and economic support systems.

In conclusion, the economic recovery and development efforts following the Korean War were instrumental in shaping the modern history of the Korean Peninsula. The contrasting paths taken by North and South Korea, the influence of external powers, and the long-term consequences on international relations and human rights all highlight the significance of understanding the economic aspects of this forgotten conflict. By examining these overlooked dimensions, historians can gain a more comprehensive understanding of the enduring impact of the Korean War.

Economic Disparities between North and South Korea

The economic disparities between North and South Korea have been a prominent and enduring consequence of the Korean War. This subchapter aims to explore the significant differences in economic development and living standards that emerged between the two countries following the war.

The Korean War, which lasted from 1950 to 1953, resulted in the division of Korea into two separate nations along the 38th parallel. The North, led by Kim Il-sung, adopted a communist ideology and received substantial economic aid from the Soviet Union and China. In contrast, the South, under the leadership of Syngman Rhee, embraced capitalism and received assistance from the United States and other Western nations.

The economic consequences of the war were stark. South Korea, with support from the United States and a focus on industrialization, experienced rapid economic growth known as the "Miracle on the Han River." The country implemented market-oriented policies, attracted foreign investment, and developed industries such as electronics, automobiles, and shipbuilding. As a result, South Korea's economy flourished, and it became one of the world's leading export-oriented economies.

In contrast, North Korea's economy struggled due to its isolationist policies and heavy reliance on centrally planned economic systems. The country focused on heavy industries and military expenditures, neglecting agriculture and consumer goods production. This approach, combined with economic mismanagement and international sanctions, resulted in chronic food shortages, economic stagnation, and poverty for the North Korean population.

The economic disparities between the two Koreas became increasingly evident over time. By the 1970s, South Korea's per capita income had surpassed that of North Korea by a significant margin. Today, South Korea boasts a thriving economy, advanced technology, and high living standards. In contrast, North Korea remains one of the world's poorest and most isolated nations, heavily dependent on foreign aid and faced with ongoing economic challenges.

The economic disparities between North and South Korea continue to shape the geopolitical landscape of the Korean Peninsula and have significant implications for international relations. Understanding these disparities and their historical roots is crucial for historians studying the long-lasting impact of the Korean War on the region.

In conclusion, the economic disparities between North and South Korea have been a defining consequence of the Korean War. South Korea's rapid economic growth and development, coupled with North Korea's economic struggles, have created stark differences in living standards and economic opportunities between the two countries. These disparities continue to shape the history, geopolitics, and international relations of the Korean Peninsula.

Global Economic Implications

The Korean War, often referred to as the "Forgotten Conflict," had far-reaching economic consequences that continue to impact the world today. This subchapter delves into the various ways in which the conflict shaped global economies, both during and after the war.

During the Korean War, the economic implications were felt not only in the countries directly involved but also across the world. The war disrupted global trade and caused significant economic instability. The conflict led to the destruction of infrastructure, factories, and agricultural land, resulting in a severe economic downturn in both North and South Korea. The Korean Peninsula's division further exacerbated this economic crisis, as trade between the two regions came to a halt.

The role of external powers in the Korean War had a profound impact on the global economy. The United States and the Soviet Union, as the main actors supporting different sides of the conflict, provided economic aid to their respective allies. This aid not only influenced the outcome of the war but also shaped the economic trajectory of these countries in the long run. The United States, in particular, saw the Korean War as an opportunity to showcase its economic prowess and establish itself as a global superpower.

The economic consequences of the Korean War were not limited to the countries directly involved. The war disrupted global supply chains and caused inflation, particularly in the United States, as resources were redirected towards the war effort. Additionally, the war fueled fears of communist expansion, leading to increased military spending in many countries. This arms race further strained global economies and diverted resources away from much-needed development projects.

The economic impact of the Korean War also had long-lasting effects on international relations and geopolitics. The war solidified the division between the communist and capitalist blocs, setting the stage for the Cold War. It also led to the establishment of the United Nations Command, which played a crucial role in the war and continues to be involved in maintaining peace and stability in the region.

In conclusion, the economic consequences of the Korean War were vast and far-reaching. The conflict disrupted global trade, caused economic instability, and shaped the geopolitical landscape of the time. The scars of the war continue to impact the economies of the countries involved and serve as a reminder of the enduring legacy of the Korean War on history.

Chapter 10: The Role of the United Nations in the Korean War

UN's Involvement and Mandate

The United Nations (UN) played a crucial role in the Korean War, acting as a mediator and facilitator of peace negotiations throughout the conflict. This subchapter will explore the UN's involvement and mandate during this significant period in history.

At the outbreak of the war in June 1950, the UN swiftly condemned North Korea's invasion of South Korea and called for an immediate ceasefire. The Security Council, with the support of its member states, authorized the establishment of a UN Command to repel the aggression and restore peace on the Korean Peninsula. Led by General Douglas MacArthur, this multinational force primarily consisted of troops from the United States, but also included contributions from other UN member states such as the United Kingdom, Canada, Australia, and many others.

The UN's mandate extended beyond military intervention. The organization aimed to facilitate negotiations and find a peaceful resolution to the conflict. In this endeavor, the UN sponsored several rounds of talks between the warring parties, including the famous Panmunjom negotiations, which resulted in the signing of the Korean Armistice Agreement in July 1953. This agreement effectively ended the hostilities, but it did not lead to a final peace treaty, leaving the Korean Peninsula divided into the communist North and the capitalist South.

The UN's involvement in the Korean War had profound implications for international relations and geopolitics. It marked the first major military action undertaken by the organization, highlighting its commitment to maintaining peace and security globally. The war also showcased the influence of external powers, particularly the United States and the Soviet Union, who supported opposing sides in the conflict. This rivalry between the superpowers further exacerbated tensions and contributed to the prolonged division of Korea.

Furthermore, the UN's involvement in the Korean War raised concerns about human rights violations. Both sides engaged in brutal acts, including mass killings, torture, and forced labor. The UN established a Commission on Human Rights to investigate these abuses, shedding light on the atrocities committed during the war and further emphasizing the importance of protecting human rights in future conflicts.

In conclusion, the UN's involvement and mandate during the Korean War were multifaceted. The organization played a vital role in both military intervention and peace negotiations, reflecting its commitment to maintaining global peace and security. However, the war's enduring impact on history extends beyond its military aspects, with implications for human rights, international relations, and the division of the Korean Peninsula. Understanding the UN's involvement in this conflict is crucial for historians and scholars studying the Korean War's lasting consequences.

UN's Peacekeeping Efforts

The United Nations (UN) played a crucial role in the Korean War, particularly through its peacekeeping efforts aimed at resolving the conflict and restoring peace on the Korean Peninsula. This subchapter explores the UN's involvement, its challenges, and its lasting impact on history.

From the onset of the war in 1950, the UN demonstrated its commitment to international peace and security by swiftly responding to the North Korean invasion of South Korea. The UN Security Council, under the leadership of the United States, passed resolutions condemning the aggression and calling for member states to provide military assistance to South Korea. This marked the first time that the UN invoked the collective security principle outlined in its charter.

With the formation of the UN Command, under the leadership of General Douglas MacArthur, a multinational force was assembled to repel North Korean forces and restore peace. Troops from various countries, including the United States, United Kingdom, Canada, and Australia, were deployed to support South Korea's defense. The UN Command's efforts proved crucial in pushing back North Korean forces and preventing the complete takeover of the peninsula.

However, the UN's peacekeeping mission faced numerous challenges throughout the conflict. The involvement of external powers, particularly China, complicated efforts to reach a peaceful resolution. The Chinese People's Volunteer Army's intervention on behalf of North Korea led to a stalemate and prolonged the war. Despite these challenges, the UN maintained its commitment to peace and continued its efforts to negotiate a ceasefire.

In 1953, the UN finally achieved a breakthrough when the Armistice Agreement was signed, effectively ending the active fighting. The agreement established a demilitarized zone along the 38th parallel, which continues to divide North and South Korea to this day. The UN's peacekeeping efforts were instrumental in bringing an end to the conflict, albeit without a formal peace treaty.

The UN's role in the Korean War had a lasting impact on international relations and geopolitics. The conflict highlighted the UN's ability to mobilize international support for peacekeeping operations and marked a turning point in its history. It also demonstrated the influence of external powers in regional conflicts and the complexities of Cold War politics.

Furthermore, the Korean War raised significant human rights concerns, with both sides accused of committing atrocities and violating the rights of civilians and prisoners of war. The UN's presence and subsequent investigation into these violations shed light on the human rights abuses that occurred during the conflict.

In conclusion, the UN's peacekeeping efforts during the Korean War were pivotal in resolving the conflict and restoring peace on the Korean Peninsula. Its involvement showcased the organization's commitment to international peace and security, while also highlighting the challenges posed by external powers and the complexities of the Cold War. The legacy of the UN's role in the Korean War continues to shape international relations, geopolitics, and discussions surrounding human rights violations.

Challenges and Criticisms of the UN's Role

The United Nations (UN) played a significant role in the Korean War, but its involvement was not without challenges and criticisms. Historians studying this conflict have identified several key issues that affected the UN's effectiveness and raised concerns about its role.

One major challenge was the lack of unity among UN member states regarding the Korean War. While the UN Security Council authorized military intervention to repel North Korean aggression, some member states, such as the Soviet Union, boycotted the decision, limiting the UN's ability to act decisively. This lack of consensus weakened the UN's credibility and hindered its ability to achieve a swift resolution to the conflict.

Critics also argue that the UN's military strategy during the war was flawed. The decision to primarily rely on air power and limited ground operations, while avoiding a full-scale invasion of North Korea, prolonged the conflict and resulted in high casualties on both sides.

Some historians believe that a more aggressive approach could have brought about a quicker end to the war, sparing countless lives.

Another criticism of the UN's role in the Korean War is the alleged bias in its decision-making process. Critics argue that the UN, particularly the United States, prioritized its own geopolitical interests over the well-being of the Korean people. This perception was further reinforced by the UN's silence on human rights violations committed by both North and South Korean forces during the war.

The UN's failure to negotiate a lasting peace settlement is also a subject of criticism. Despite numerous attempts to negotiate a ceasefire, the war ultimately ended in an armistice, leaving the Korean Peninsula divided and technically still at war. Critics argue that the UN's inability to bring about a formal peace agreement has perpetuated the enduring tensions between North and South Korea and has contributed to the region's ongoing instability.

Overall, while the UN's involvement in the Korean War was a landmark moment in its history, it faced significant challenges and criticisms. These include the lack of unity among member states, flawed military strategy, perceived bias, failure to address human rights violations, and the absence of a lasting peace settlement. Understanding these challenges and criticisms is crucial for historians studying the Korean War and its enduring impact on history.

The UN's Legacy in Conflict Resolution

The Korean War, often referred to as the "Forgotten Conflict," holds a significant place in history due to its enduring impact on various aspects of global affairs. One crucial element that cannot be overlooked is the role played by the United Nations (UN) in the resolution of the conflict. This subchapter delves into the UN's legacy in conflict resolution, highlighting its efforts to bring about peace and stability on the Korean Peninsula.

The UN's involvement in the Korean War marked a watershed moment in the organization's history. It was the first time the UN had actively engaged in a military conflict, demonstrating its commitment to maintaining international peace and security. The decision to intervene in Korea, under the auspices of the UN Security Council, set a precedent for future peacekeeping missions.

Throughout the war, the UN played a pivotal role in mediating between the warring parties, striving to find a diplomatic solution to the conflict. The organization's constant diplomatic efforts, led by diplomats from various member states, aimed to bring about a ceasefire and negotiate a lasting peace settlement. Despite the challenges and complexities, the UN's involvement helped prevent the complete collapse of negotiations and paved the way for future diplomatic initiatives.

Moreover, the UN's legacy in conflict resolution extends beyond the duration of the war itself. The organization's presence in post-war Korea was instrumental in ensuring stability and facilitating the reconstruction process. The United Nations Command, established during the war, transitioned into overseeing the armistice agreement and maintaining peace along the demilitarized zone. This ongoing UN presence has served as a deterrent to further hostilities and has contributed to the relative peace enjoyed on the Korean Peninsula since the armistice was signed.

The UN's legacy in conflict resolution during the Korean War also had broader implications for international relations and geopolitics. The successful UN-led intervention in Korea demonstrated the organization's ability to address global conflicts and foster cooperation among member states. It highlighted the importance of multilateralism in resolving complex issues and solidified the UN's role as a global peacekeeper.

In conclusion, the UN's legacy in conflict resolution during the Korean War is a testament to its commitment to maintaining international peace and security. Through its diplomatic efforts, peacekeeping missions, and ongoing presence on the Korean Peninsula, the UN has played a crucial role in preventing the resumption of hostilities and fostering stability. The organization's involvement in the Korean War has left an indelible mark on international relations, demonstrating the efficacy of multilateral approaches to resolving conflicts and shaping the course of history.

Chapter 11: Human Rights Violations during the Korean War

Massacres and Atrocities

The chapter "Massacres and Atrocities" delves deep into the horrifying events that unfolded during the Korean War, shining a light on the dark side of this forgotten conflict. This subchapter aims to provide a comprehensive understanding of the various massacres and atrocities committed by all parties involved, leaving no stone unturned in its exploration of this tragic aspect of history.

The Korean War witnessed a series of massacres and atrocities that resulted in the loss of countless innocent lives. From the No Gun Ri Massacre, where American soldiers killed numerous South Korean civilians, to the Bodo League Massacre, where thousands of suspected communists were executed by South Korean forces, the bloodshed was relentless.

These events were not confined to one side of the conflict. The North Korean and Chinese forces were also responsible for their share of atrocities, such as the Sinchon Massacre, where it is believed that thousands of civilians were brutally murdered by communist forces.

The subchapter also examines the role of propaganda in fueling these massacres and atrocities. Propaganda played a significant role in dehumanizing the enemy, creating an environment where violence and brutality were normalized. The impact of propaganda on both soldiers and civilians cannot be underestimated, as it shaped their perceptions and fueled the cycle of violence.

Furthermore, the subchapter delves into the human rights violations that occurred during the Korean War. From forced labor and sexual violence to torture and arbitrary executions, these violations left an indelible mark on the victims and their families. The chapter sheds light on these atrocities, ensuring that their memory is not forgotten.

Ultimately, "Massacres and Atrocities" provides a comprehensive overview of the darkest aspects of the Korean War. It addresses the experiences of both soldiers and civilians, shedding light on the horrors they endured. By examining the role of propaganda, the subchapter also offers insights into the psychological and societal factors that contributed to these atrocities.

This subchapter is a vital resource for historians and those interested in understanding the full impact of the Korean War. By uncovering these forgotten stories, it contributes to a more comprehensive understanding of the war's enduring impact on history, international relations, and geopolitics.

Displacement and Refugee Crisis

The Korean War, often referred to as "The Forgotten Conflict," was not only a brutal and deadly war but also a humanitarian crisis that resulted in a massive displacement of people and a refugee crisis. This subchapter delves into the experiences of those who were forced to flee their homes, the challenges they faced, and the long-lasting impact of this crisis on the Korean Peninsula.

During the Korean War, which lasted from 1950 to 1953, millions of Koreans were uprooted from their homes due to the violent conflict between North and South Korea. As the war raged on, entire villages and cities were destroyed, leaving countless families with no choice but to flee to safer areas. The majority of these displaced individuals were women, children, and the elderly, who often lacked essential resources and faced numerous hardships on their journey.

The refugee crisis during the Korean War was further exacerbated by the involvement of external powers. With the United States supporting South Korea and China backing North Korea, the conflict became a proxy war that attracted international attention. As a result, neighboring countries such as Japan, China, and the Soviet Union were also affected by the influx of Korean refugees seeking safety and aid.

The experiences of Korean prisoners of war (POWs) during and after the war were also closely tied to the displacement crisis. Many POWs faced immense challenges while in captivity, enduring harsh conditions, torture, and even death. After the war, those who managed to survive the ordeal often struggled to reintegrate into society and rebuild their lives.

The displacement and refugee crisis had a profound impact on the Korean Peninsula's division. The war not only hardened the borders between North and South Korea but also created a stark contrast in terms of economic development and political ideologies. The division caused by the war continues to shape the geopolitical landscape of the region and has had far-reaching implications on international relations.

Furthermore, the displacement crisis led to significant cultural and societal changes in both North and South Korea. The war disrupted traditional family structures and social norms, with women taking on new roles and responsibilities in the absence of male family members. The war also had a lasting impact on the economy, with both countries facing significant challenges in rebuilding and recovering from the devastation.

As historians, it is crucial to examine the displacement and refugee crisis during the Korean War to fully understand the war's enduring impact on history. By exploring the experiences of those affected, we gain valuable insights into the profound human suffering caused by war and the lasting consequences it has on individuals, societies, and international relations. Additionally, shedding light on the displacement crisis allows us to recognize the human rights violations that occurred during the Korean War and work towards preventing such atrocities in the future.

Prison Camps and Forced Labor

The Korean War was not just a conflict between the two Koreas and their respective allies, but it also witnessed numerous human rights violations that have had a lasting impact on history. One of the most disturbing aspects of this war was the existence of prison camps and the use of forced labor by both sides.

Prison camps were established by both North Korea and South Korea during the war, where prisoners of war (POWs) were held captive under appalling conditions. These camps became sites of unimaginable suffering, where prisoners were subjected to physical and psychological torture, starvation, and disease. The prisoners were often denied basic necessities such as food, clean water, and medical care, leading to high mortality rates.

Forced labor was another widespread practice during the Korean War. Both sides exploited prisoners and civilians, forcing them to work long hours under harsh conditions. Prisoners and civilians were often used in industries such as mining, agriculture, and construction, contributing to the war efforts of their captors. Many of these workers were subjected to physical abuse and were not provided with adequate protection or compensation for their labor.

These prison camps and forced labor practices had a profound impact on the Korean Peninsula's division and the experiences of the people involved. The use of such inhumane tactics further deepened the divide between North and South Korea, fueling animosity and resentment that still exists today. The experiences of Korean POWs during and after the war shaped their perceptions and had lasting effects on their lives and the societies they returned to.

Furthermore, these human rights violations also had implications for international relations and geopolitics. The existence of prison camps and forced labor became a contentious issue, with reports of such atrocities reaching the international community. This raised questions about the role of external powers in the Korean War and their responsibility in addressing these violations. It also highlighted the importance of human rights in shaping the legacy of the war and its impact on global politics.

The prison camps and forced labor during the Korean War also had significant economic consequences. The exploitation of labor and resources contributed to the destruction of infrastructure and disrupted the normal functioning of industries in both North and South Korea. The long-term effects of this are still felt today, as the economic development of the Korean Peninsula was hindered by the war and its aftermath.

In conclusion, the existence of prison camps and forced labor during the Korean War is a dark chapter in history that deserves attention. The experiences of the prisoners, the societal changes in the post-war era, and the long-lasting impact on international relations, geopolitics, and the economy highlight the enduring consequences of these human rights violations. Understanding and acknowledging these atrocities is crucial for historians studying the Korean War and its multifaceted impacts.

Truth and Reconciliation Efforts

In the aftermath of the devastating Korean War, efforts were made to foster truth and reconciliation among the conflicting parties. The war, which lasted from 1950 to 1953, not only caused immense human suffering but also left lasting scars on the Korean Peninsula. These scars were not only physical, but also emotional and psychological, as families were torn apart, cities were reduced to rubble, and deep-rooted animosities were formed.

Truth and reconciliation efforts aimed to address the painful memories and grievances of those affected by the war, while also working towards healing and rebuilding a fractured nation. One of the key elements of these efforts was the establishment of truth commissions, which were tasked with investigating and documenting the atrocities committed during the war. These commissions sought to uncover the truth about the war, including the human rights violations that took place, in order to bring about a sense of justice and closure.

The truth commissions played a crucial role in uncovering the extent of the suffering experienced by both sides of the conflict. They provided a platform for victims to share their stories, ensuring that their voices were heard and their experiences validated. By acknowledging the pain and suffering endured by all parties involved, these truth and reconciliation efforts aimed to promote empathy and understanding among the divided Korean people.

Furthermore, truth and reconciliation efforts also sought to foster dialogue and promote reconciliation between North and South Korea. Despite the armistice agreement signed in 1953, the two sides remained deeply divided, with tensions often escalating. The truth commissions provided a forum for open and honest discussions about the war, encouraging a shared understanding of the past and facilitating the process of reconciliation.

While truth and reconciliation efforts have made significant progress in addressing the wounds of the Korean War, challenges remain. The deeply entrenched political divisions and ongoing conflicts between North and South Korea have hindered the full realization of reconciliation. However, the importance of these efforts cannot be understated, as they provide a foundation for future peacebuilding and understanding.

In conclusion, truth and reconciliation efforts have played a crucial role in addressing the enduring impact of the Korean War. By uncovering the truth, promoting dialogue, and fostering reconciliation, these efforts have attempted to heal the wounds of the past and pave the way for a more peaceful and unified future on the Korean Peninsula. As historians, it is our duty to continue studying and documenting these efforts, in order to understand their impact on history and ensure that the lessons learned from the Korean War are not forgotten.

Conclusion: The Enduring Impact of the Forgotten Conflict

The Korean War may be labeled as the "Forgotten Conflict," but its impact on history has been enduring and far-reaching. Throughout this book, we have explored various aspects of the war and its aftermath, shedding light on its significance and the lessons we can learn from it. From the war's role in ongoing tensions on the Korean Peninsula to the influence of external powers, the experiences of POWs, and the cultural and societal changes in North and South Korea, it is clear that the Korean War has left an indelible mark on history.

One of the key findings in our exploration is the war's ongoing impact on the division of the Korean Peninsula. Despite the armistice signed in 1953, the war has not officially ended, and tensions persist between North and South Korea. This division has had profound consequences for the people living on both sides, causing economic disparities, political instability, and a constant state of uncertainty.

Propaganda played a significant role in the Korean War, shaping public opinion and influencing the course of the conflict. Both sides utilized propaganda to rally support for their cause, demonize the enemy, and maintain morale. Understanding the role of propaganda allows us to delve deeper into the complexities of the war and its lasting effects on the perceptions and attitudes of the Korean people.

The Korean War also highlights the influence of external powers on regional conflicts. With the intervention of the United States, China, and the Soviet Union, the war became a proxy battleground for the larger Cold War struggle. The involvement of these global powers not only prolonged the conflict but also shaped the geopolitical landscape of the region, setting the stage for future tensions and rivalries.

The experiences of Korean POWs during and after the war provide a sobering reminder of the human cost of the conflict. Many endured unimaginable hardships, both physical and psychological, and their stories offer valuable insights into the realities of war and its long-term effects on individuals and societies.

Post-war, both North and South Korea underwent significant cultural and societal changes. North Korea embraced an ideology centered around the cult of personality, while South Korea pursued rapid industrialization and economic growth. These divergent paths have created distinct societies with differing values, beliefs, and aspirations.

The legacy of the Korean War also extends to international relations and geopolitics. The war solidified the United States' commitment to containing communism and defending its allies, leading to a more interventionist foreign policy. It also highlighted the limitations of the United Nations as a peacekeeping body and sparked debates about its effectiveness in resolving conflicts.

The economic consequences of the Korean War were immense, with both North and South Korea suffering significant setbacks. The war left behind a devastated infrastructure, disrupted agriculture, and displaced populations, setting the stage for economic struggles that would persist for decades.

Finally, the Korean War exposed numerous human rights violations, including mass executions, forced labor, and sexual violence. These violations, often overshadowed by the larger geopolitical context, deserve attention and serve as reminders of the atrocities committed during times of war.

In conclusion, the Korean War's enduring impact on history cannot be underestimated. From the ongoing division of the Korean Peninsula to the role of propaganda, external powers, POW experiences, cultural and societal changes, and the economic, geopolitical, and human rights implications, this forgotten conflict continues to shape our world today. As historians, it is our responsibility to delve deeper into the complexities of this war and ensure that its lessons are not forgotten but rather used to inform our understanding of the past, the present, and the future.